CW00674575

PRINCE2® Handbook

part of Williams Lea Tag

Published by TSO (The Stationery Office), part of Williams Lea, and available from:

Online
www.tsoshop.co.uk

Mail, Telephone, Fax & E-mail
TSO
PO Box 29, Norwich, NR3 1GN
Telephone orders/General enquiries: 0333 202 5070
Fax orders: 0333 202 5080
E-mail: customer.services@tso.co.uk
Textphone 0333 202 5077

TSO@Blackwell and other Accredited Agents

First edition 2017
ISBN 9780113315420

Printed in the United Kingdom for The Stationery Office
Material is FSC certified and produced using ECF pulp, sourced from fully sustainable forests.

P002918137   c3   01/18

Contents

About AXELOS

AXELOS is a joint venture company co-owned by the UK Government's Cabinet Office and Capita plc. It is responsible for developing, enhancing and promoting a number of best-practice methodologies used globally by professionals working primarily in project, programme and portfolio management, IT service management and cyber resilience.

The methodologies, including ITIL®, PRINCE2®, MSP® and the new collection of cyber resilience best-practice products, RESILIA™, are adopted in more than 150 countries to improve employees' skills, knowledge and competence in order to make both individuals and organizations work more effectively.

In addition to globally recognized qualifications, AXELOS equips professionals with a wide range of content, templates and toolkits through its membership scheme, its professional development programme and its online community of practitioners and experts.

Visit www.axelos.com for the latest news about how AXELOS is making organizations more effective and registration details to join the AXELOS online community. If you have specific queries or requests, or would like to be added to the AXELOS mailing list, please contact ask@axelos.com.

Publications

AXELOS publishes a comprehensive range of guidance, including *Managing Successful Projects with PRINCE2®*, which provides more detailed information on using PRINCE2. Other AXELOS publications include:

- *PRINCE2 Agile®*
- *Integrating PRINCE2®*
- *Directing Successful Projects with PRINCE2®*
- *Management of Portfolios* (MoP®)

- *Managing Successful Programmes* (MSP®)
- *Management of Risk: Guidance for Practitioners* (M_o_R®)
- *Portfolio, Programme and Project Offices* (P3O®)
- Portfolio, Programme and Project Management Maturity Model (P3M3®)
- *Management of Value* (MoV®)
- *RESILIA™: Cyber Resilience Best Practice*
- IT service management publications (ITIL®).

Full details of the range of materials published under the AXELOS Global Best Practice banner, including *PRINCE2 Handbook*, can be found at:

https://www.axelos.com/best-practice-solutions

If you would like to inform AXELOS of any changes that may be required to *PRINCE2 Handbook* or any other AXELOS publication, please log them at:

https://www.axelos.com/best-practice-feedback

Contact information

Full details on how to contact AXELOS can be found at:

https://www.axelos.com

For further information on qualifications and training accreditation, please visit:

https://www.axelos.com/qualifications

https://www.axelos.com/training-organization-benefits

For all other enquiries, please email:

ask@axelos.com

Acknowledgements

Following the 2017 update of *Managing Successful Projects with PRINCE2*, this handbook was compiled by Mike Acaster, Neil Glover and Allan Thomson. Mike, Neil and Allan are all members of the AXELOS project team.

AXELOS Ltd is grateful to Andy Murray (RSM UK) and Michelle Rowland (A&J Project Management Ltd) for providing review comments.

1 Introduction

1.1 What is PRINCE2®?

PRINCE2 (PRojects IN Controlled Environments) is one of the most widely used methods for managing projects in the world. It is a structured project management method based on experience drawn from thousands of projects and from the contributions of countless project sponsors, project managers, project teams, academics, trainers and consultants.

PRINCE2 has been designed to be generic so that it can be applied to any project, regardless of project environment, scale, type, organization, geography or culture. It achieves this by:

● separating the management of project work from the specialist contributions, such as design or construction. The specialist aspects of any type of project are easily integrated with the PRINCE2 method and, used alongside PRINCE2, provide a secure overall framework for the project work.

● focusing on describing what needs to be done, rather than prescribing how everything is done.

The value of PRINCE2 is that it can be used on any project because the method is designed to be tailored to meet the specific needs of the organization and scaled to the size and complexity of individual projects.

The purpose of tailoring PRINCE2 is to ensure that:

● the project management method used is appropriate to the project (e.g. aligning the method with the business processes that may govern and support the project, such as human resources, finance and procurement)

- project controls are appropriate to the project's scale, complexity, importance, team capability and risk (e.g. the frequency and formality of reports and reviews).

Because PRINCE2 is based on proven principles, organizations adopting the method as a standard can substantially improve their organizational capability and maturity across multiple areas of business activity, such as business change, construction, IT, mergers and acquisitions, research and product development.

1.2 The importance of projects

A key challenge for organizations in today's world is to succeed in balancing two parallel, competing imperatives. These are to:

- maintain current business operations (i.e. profitability, service quality, customer relationships, brand loyalty, productivity, market confidence, etc.). This is what we would term 'business as usual'
- transform business operations, or introduce new products, in order to survive and compete in the future (i.e. looking forward and deciding how business change can be introduced to best effect for the organization).

As the pace of change accelerates (in technology, business, society, regulation, etc.), and the penalties of failing to adapt to change become more evident, the focus of management attention inevitably moves to achieve a balance between business as usual and business change.

Projects are the means by which we introduce change and, although many of the skills required are the same, there are some crucial differences between managing business as usual and managing project work.

1.3 What makes projects different?

A project is a temporary organization that is created for the purpose of delivering one or more business products according to an agreed business case.

There are a number of characteristics of project work that distinguish it from business as usual:

- **Change** Projects are the means by which we introduce change.

- **Temporary** As already stated, projects are temporary in nature. When the desired change has been implemented, business as usual resumes (in its new form) and the need for the project is removed. Projects should have a defined start and a defined end.

- **Cross-functional** Projects involve a team of people with different skills working together (on a temporary basis) to introduce a change that will impact others outside the team. Projects often cross the normal functional divisions within an organization and sometimes span entirely different organizations. This frequently causes stresses and strains both within organizations and between them (for example, between customers and suppliers). Each has a different perspective and motivation for getting involved in the change.

- **Unique** Every project is unique. An organization may undertake many similar projects and establish a familiar, proven pattern of project activity, but each project will be unique in some way: a different team, a different customer, a different location. All these factors combine to make every project unique.

- **Uncertainty** Clearly, the characteristics already listed will introduce threats and opportunities over and above those we typically encounter in the course of business as usual. Projects are more risky.

1.4 Why have a project management method?

Project management is the planning, delegating, monitoring and control of all aspects of the project, and the motivation of those involved, to achieve the project objectives within the expected performance targets for time, cost, quality, scope, benefits and risk.

For example, a new house is completed by creating drawings, foundations, floors, walls, windows, a roof, plumbing, wiring and connected services. None of this is project management, so why do we need project management at all? The purpose of project management is to keep control over the specialist work required to create the project's products or, to continue with the house analogy, to make sure the roofing contractor does not arrive before the walls are built.

Additionally, given that projects are the means by which we introduce a change, and that project work entails a higher degree of risk than many other business activities, it follows that implementing a secure, consistent, well-proven approach to project management is a valuable business investment.

Increased business performance through the effective use of project management methods across organizations has been demonstrated through the use of maturity assessments. These measure an organization's capability to manage projects, programmes and/or portfolios. Maturity assessments can be undertaken using the AXELOS Portfolio, Programme and Project Management Maturity Model (P3M3®).

1.5 The role of senior management

The project management structure has four levels, three of which represent the project management team and a fourth that sits outside the project. Figure 1.1 illustrates these four levels of management.

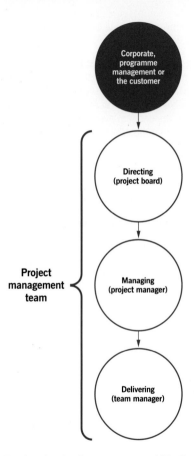

Figure 1.1 The four levels of management within the project management structure

PRINCE2 enables effective governance by defining distinct responsibilities for each of these levels.

The project board represents the most senior level of management within the PRINCE2 project management team. Project board members are accountable for the work they direct, but the extent of their business responsibilities is usually much wider than the project. They can rarely afford to get involved in the detail of every project for which they are responsible. This means that the effectiveness with which they delegate responsibility for the different aspects of the project is crucial.

In PRINCE2, the project board delegates the management of the project to the project manager in a series of stages, each based on an approved stage plan. Provided that the project manager can deliver the stage within the tolerances defined in the plan, there is no necessity for the project board members to maintain close contact with the work. Should the project manager forecast that the tolerances will be exceeded, however, the project board will be alerted through an exception report. The project board will then review and approve the options for addressing the exception.

The stage boundaries represent major control milestones, enabling the project board to review whether the project manager has delivered the previous stage properly and to approve a plan for the succeeding stage. The PRINCE2 processes provide other checks and balances within the stage but, essentially, this is how senior managers on the project board are able to 'manage by exception'.

To fully understand the project board's responsibilities, it is important to be aware of the underlying duties and the behaviours that are expected of the board members (see Figure 1.2). Why is this important? Because lack of executive/senior management support is frequently cited as one of the top causes of project failure.

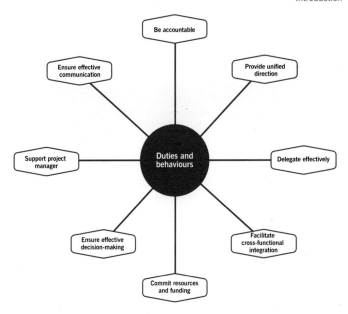

Figure 1.2 Project board duties and behaviours

Senior managers acting as project board members must provide leadership and direction to ensure that their projects remain aligned with the organization's strategic aims. The project board is seen as a guiding coalition and, together with the project manager, they must make proactive choices and decisions on how PRINCE2 will be tailored for the project. Effective tailoring requires information (not necessarily documents) and good decisions (not necessarily meetings).

As with company boards, if the composition of the project board is deficient in the required skills and behaviours, then the project is likely to struggle (for example, if the project board is affected by personality clashes and in-fighting).

Key message

Appointing the right project board is probably the single most important factor in achieving a successful project.

1.6 What does a project manager do?

In order to achieve control over anything, there must be a plan. For example, when building a house, it is the project manager who is responsible for planning the sequence of activities, working out how many bricklayers will be required, and so on.

It may be possible to build the house yourself, but being a manager implies that you will delegate some or all of the work to others. The ability to delegate is important in any form of management but particularly so in project management, because of the cross-functionality and the risks involved.

With the delegated work under way, the aim is that it should 'go according to plan', but we cannot rely on this always being the case. It is the project manager's responsibility to monitor how well the work in progress matches the plan's objectives (see Figure 1.3).

Of course, if the work does not go according to plan, the project manager has to do something about it, i.e. exert control. Even if the work is going well, the project manager may identify an opportunity to speed it up or reduce costs.

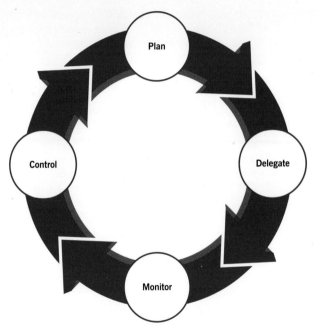

Figure 1.3 Project management

Key message

One aim of PRINCE2 is to make the right information available at the right time for the right people to make the right decisions about the project. Those decisions include whether to take corrective action or implement measures to improve performance.

1.7 What is it we wish to control?

There are six variables involved in any project, and therefore six aspects of project performance to be managed. These are:

- **Costs** The project has to be affordable and, though we may start out with a particular budget in mind, there will be many factors which can lead to overspending and, perhaps, some opportunities to cut costs.

- **Timescales** Closely linked to this, and probably one of the questions project managers are most frequently asked, is: 'When will it be finished?'

- **Quality** Finishing on time and within budget is not much consolation if the result of the project does not work. In PRINCE2 terms, the project's products must be fit for purpose.

- **Scope** Exactly what will the project deliver? Without knowing it, the various parties involved in a project can very often be talking at cross-purposes about this. The customer may assume that, for instance, a fitted kitchen and/or bathroom is included in the price of the house, whereas the supplier views these as 'extras'. On large-scale projects, scope definition is much more subtle and complex. There must be agreement on the project's scope and the project manager needs to have a sufficient understanding of what is and what is not within the scope. The project manager should take care not to deliver beyond the scope as this is a common source of delays, overspends and uncontrolled change ('scope creep').

● **Benefits** Perhaps most often overlooked is the question: Why are we doing this? It is not enough to build the house successfully on time, within budget and to quality specifications if, in the end, we cannot sell or rent it at a profit or live in it happily. The project manager has to have a clear understanding of the purpose of the project as an investment and make sure that what the project delivers is consistent with achieving the desired return.

● **Risk** All projects entail risks but exactly how much risk are we prepared to accept? Should we build the house near the site of a disused mine, which may be prone to subsidence? If we decide to go ahead, is there something we can do about the risk? Maybe insure against it, enhance (underpin) the house foundations or simply monitor with ongoing surveys?

PRINCE2 addresses the planning, delegation, monitoring and control of all these six aspects of project performance.

1.8 The structure of PRINCE2

The PRINCE2 method addresses project management with four integrated elements of principles, themes, processes and the project environment (Figure 1.4):

● **PRINCE2 principles** These are the guiding obligations and good practices which determine whether the project is genuinely being managed using PRINCE2. There are seven principles and unless all of them are applied, it is not a PRINCE2 project.

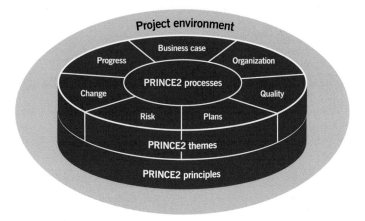

Figure 1.4 The structure of PRINCE2

PRINCE2 is a flexible method and one of the principles is that it should be tailored to the type and size of project.

- **PRINCE2 themes** These are aspects of project management that must be addressed continually and in parallel throughout the project. The seven themes explain the specific treatment required by PRINCE2 for various project management disciplines and why they are necessary.

- **PRINCE2 processes** These describe a progression through the project lifecycle, from getting started to project closure. Each process provides checklists of recommended activities, products and related responsibilities.

● **The project environment** Organizations often want a consistent approach to managing projects and will tailor PRINCE2 to create their own project management method. This method is then embedded into the organization's way of working.

 Key message

For a project to be following PRINCE2, as a minimum it must be possible to demonstrate that the project:

● is applying PRINCE2's principles

● is meeting the minimum requirements set out in the PRINCE2 themes

● has project processes that satisfy the purpose and objectives of the PRINCE2 processes

● is either using PRINCE2's recommended techniques or using alternative, equivalent techniques.

1.9 Projects in context

PRINCE2 assumes that there will be a customer who will specify the desired result and a supplier who will provide the resources and skills to deliver that result. PRINCE2 refers to:

● the organization that commissions a project as 'corporate, programme management or the customer'. This organization is responsible for providing the project's mandate, governing the project, and for realizing any benefits that the project might deliver or enable.

● a supplier as the person, group or groups responsible for the supply of the project's specialist products.

Projects can exist within many contexts; they may be stand-alone (with their own business case and justification) or they may be part of a programme or wider portfolio as illustrated by Figure 1.5. In addition, projects may be wholly managed within the commissioning organization or be part of a commercial relationship.

Figure 1.5 Projects in the context of portfolios and programmes

1.10 PRINCE2 and delivery approaches

The project approach is the way in which the work of the project is to be delivered. It may rely on one or more delivery approaches, which are the specialist approaches used by work packages to create the products. Typical approaches include:

● a waterfall approach where each of the delivery steps to create the products takes place in sequence (e.g. in a construction project where requirements gathering and design take place before building begins) and the product is made available during or at the end of the project

● an agile approach where requirements gathering, design, delivery and testing all take place iteratively throughout the project.

2 Principles

PRINCE2 is designed so that it can be applied to any type of project, taking account of its scale, organization, geography and culture. It is designed to contribute to the success of a project without burdening it with bureaucracy.

The PRINCE2 principles provide a framework of good practice for people involved in a project and were developed from lessons taken from both successful and failed projects. The seven principles are:

- **Continued business justification** PRINCE2 requires that there is a justifiable reason for starting the project; that justification is recorded and approved; and that it remains valid, and is revalidated, throughout the life of the project.

- **Learn from experience** PRINCE2 project teams learn from experience: lessons are sought, recorded and acted upon throughout the life of the project.

- **Defined roles and responsibilities** A PRINCE2 project has defined and agreed roles and responsibilities within an organization structure that engages the business, user and supplier stakeholder interests.

- **Manage by stages** A PRINCE2 project is planned, monitored and controlled on a stage-by-stage basis.

- **Manage by exception** A PRINCE2 project has defined tolerances for each project objective, to establish limits of delegated authority.

- **Focus on products** A PRINCE2 project focuses on the definition and delivery of products, in particular their quality requirements.

- **Tailor to suit the project** PRINCE2 is tailored to suit the project environment, size, complexity, importance, team capability and risk.

To be following PRINCE2, these principles must be adopted when managing a project. Minimum requirements set out in the themes and processes must also be satisfied. These minimum requirements describe what must be done, rather than how it is done.

The PRINCE2 principles are complementary to an agile way of working. Some are 'very much agile', such as continued business justification, learn from experience, focus on products, manage by stages, and manage by exception, the last being synonymous with giving people autonomy and empowerment. For more information, see the AXELOS guide, *PRINCE2 Agile*.

3 Tailoring

The seventh PRINCE2 principle states that PRINCE2 should be tailored
for a project's particular circumstances. The goal is to apply a level of
project management that does not overburden the project management
team but provides an appropriate level of governance and control, at an
acceptable level of risk.

Key message

Tailoring can be applied to processes, themes, roles, management
products and terminology.

If PRINCE2 is not tailored, it is unlikely that the project management
effort and approach will be appropriate for the needs of the project. This
can lead to 'mechanistic' project management at one extreme (a method
is followed without question) or 'heroic' project management at the
other (a method is not followed at all).

Organizations adopt PRINCE2 by tailoring it to their needs, often
creating their own PRINCE2-based method and then embedding its use
within their working practices.

Definition: Tailoring

Adapting a method or process to suit the situation in which it will be used.

Examples of common situations where PRINCE2 should be tailored are projects:

- that the organization perceives as straightforward and of low risk
- using an agile development approach
- involving a commercial customer and supplier relationship
- involving multiple owning organizations
- within programmes or portfolios.

Definition: Embedding

The act of making something an integral part of a bigger whole. Embedding is what an organization needs to do to adopt PRINCE2 as its corporate project management method and encourage its widespread use.

4 Themes

The PRINCE2 themes describe aspects of project management that must be addressed continually as the project progresses through its lifecycle. For example, the business justification for the project will need to be updated and revalidated throughout the project lifecycle; change will take place and risks will need to be managed.

However, the strength of PRINCE2 is the way in which the seven themes are integrated, and this is achieved because of the specific PRINCE2 treatment of each theme (i.e. they are carefully designed to link together effectively).

The seven PRINCE2 themes are:

- **Business case** Explaining why the project has come about, and how the idea has been developed
- **Organization** Describing who will be in the project management team and their responsibilities
- **Quality** Describing what quality attributes are required of the products to be delivered
- **Plans** Outlining how the project is to proceed, how much resource will be required, and when things should happen (on the basis of a series of approved plans)
- **Risk** Addressing how uncertainty will be managed – the 'what if?' scenario
- **Change** Focusing on what impact any issues (arising as a result of change) may have on the project's baseline plans and products
- **Progress** Addressing the ongoing viability of the project, monitoring its performance and determining whether and how it should proceed.

Each theme is described in more detail below, but in summary, the integrated set of PRINCE2 themes describe how:

- baselines (in the form of time, cost, quality, scope, benefits and risk) are established in the business case, quality, plans and risk themes. Managing changes to the baselines is covered by the change theme.
- the project management team monitors and controls the work as the project progresses (in the progress, quality, change and risk themes).
- the organization theme supports the other themes with a structure of roles and responsibilities that has clear paths for delegation and escalation.

Each theme contains suggestions for different tailoring options to implement the theme in practice, and identifies the minimum requirements to satisfy PRINCE2.

All the themes must be applied in a project but they should be tailored according to the risk, scale, nature and complexity of the project concerned. Tailoring enables the PRINCE2 themes to be adapted to create appropriate procedures and controls for the particular project, provided that:

- the PRINCE2 principles are upheld
- the minimum requirements in each theme are satisfied
- the purpose of each theme is not compromised.

4.1 The business case theme

Key message

The purpose of the business case theme is to establish mechanisms to judge whether the project is (and remains) desirable, viable and achievable as a means to support decision-making in its (continued) investment.

In PRINCE2, all projects must have a documented business justification. This sets out the reason for the project (its objectives) and also confirms whether the project is:

- **desirable**: the balance of costs, benefits and risks
- **viable**: able to deliver the products
- **achievable**: whether use of the products is likely to result in envisaged outcomes and resulting benefits.

The business justification is usually documented in a business case which provides the costs, benefits, expected dis-benefits, risks and timescales against which viability is justified and continually tested.

It is a PRINCE2 principle that a project must have continued business justification. This requires that the business justification is not just developed at the beginning of the project, but that it is kept under regular review and updated in response to decisions and events that might impact the desirability, viability or achievability of the project.

Figure 4.1 The development path of the business case

If the business justification ceases to be valid then the executive (see section 4.2) must halt or change the project, following review by the project board (see Figure 4.1).

To be following PRINCE2, a project must, as a minimum:

● create and maintain a business justification for the project; usually a business case (PRINCE2's continued business justification principle)

● review and update the business justification in response to decisions and events that might impact desirability, viability or achievability of the project (PRINCE2's continued business justification principle)

● define the management actions that will be put in place to ensure that the project's outcomes are achieved and confirm that the project's benefits are realized (PRINCE2's continued business justification principle)

● define and document the roles and responsibilities for the business case and benefits management (PRINCE2's defined roles and responsibilities principle)

● produce and maintain two products:

  ● business case (see section A.2)

  ● benefits management approach (see section A.1).

Continued business justification drives all decision-making by ensuring that the business objectives and benefits being sought can be realized. The business justification must be reviewed and verified:

- at the end of the starting up a project process by the project board in order to authorize project initiation based on a reasonable justification

- at the end of the initiating a project process by the project board in order to authorize the project

- as part of any impact assessment by the project manager of any new or revised issues or risks

- in tandem with an exception plan by the project board, in order to authorize the revised management stage and the continuation of the project

- at the end of each management stage by the project manager to determine whether any of the costs, timescales, risks or benefits need to be updated

- at the end of each management stage by the project board, to authorize the next management stage and the continuation of the project

- during the final management stage by the project manager, to assess the project's performance against its requirements and the likelihood that the outcomes will provide the expected benefits

- as part of the benefits review (possibly by corporate, programme management or the customer), to determine the success of the project outcomes in realizing their benefits.

It is the responsibility of the executive to assure the project's stakeholders that the project remains desirable, viable and achievable at all times.

4.2 The organization theme

 Key message

The purpose of the organization theme is to define and establish the project's structure of accountability and responsibilities.

Every project needs effective direction, management, control and communication (see section 1.5 for the role of senior management). Establishing an effective project management team structure and approach for communication at the beginning of a project, and maintaining these throughout the project's lifecycle, are essential elements of a project's success.

PRINCE2 identifies three principal categories of project stakeholders, each of which has a specific interest in, or viewpoint on, the project (see Figure 4.2). Each category of stakeholder has specific roles on the project in order to ensure that their interests are met. There may also be a wide range of other stakeholders with an interest in the project: for example, government, regulators and unions. The roles representing the stakeholders are as follows:

● **Business** The products of the project should meet a business need that justifies the investment in the project. PRINCE2 defines an executive role to represent business interests on the project.

● **User** PRINCE2 makes a distinction between the business interests and the requirements of those who will use the project's outputs. PRINCE2 defines the senior user role to represent the user interest on the project.

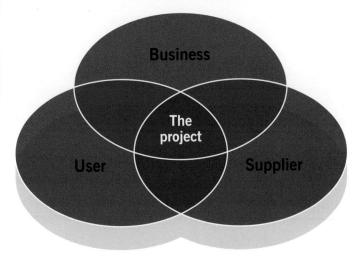

Figure 4.2 The three principal project interests

● **Supplier** The provider of the skilled resources necessary to create
the project's output (product). PRINCE2 defines a senior supplier
role to represent supplier interest on the project.

Summaries of the roles and their responsibilities can be found
in Appendix C.

Some of the PRINCE2 responsibilities cannot be shared or delegated if
they are to be undertaken effectively:

● The project manager and executive roles cannot be shared, i.e. the
executive cannot also be the project manager and there cannot be
more than one executive or project manager

● The decision-making accountability of the project manager and project board cannot be delegated.

To be following PRINCE2, a project must, as a minimum:

● define its organization structure and roles. This must minimally ensure that all of the responsibilities in PRINCE2's role descriptions are fulfilled (PRINCE2's defined roles and responsibilities principle)

● document the rules for delegating change authority responsibilities, if required

● define its approach to communicating and engaging with stakeholders

● produce and maintain two products:

  ● project initiation documentation (PID) (see section A.20)

  ● communication management approach (see section A.5).

4.3 The quality theme

Key message

The purpose of the quality theme is to define and implement the means by which the project will verify that products are fit for purpose.

Quality is concerned with ensuring that the project's products meet business expectations and enable the desired benefits to be realized.

The 'focus on products' principle is central to PRINCE2's approach to quality. It provides an explicit understanding of what the project will create (the scope) and the criteria against which the project's products will be assessed (the quality).

PRINCE2 addresses the two activities of quality planning and quality control (see Figure 4.3):

● Quality planning is about defining the project's products, with their respective quality criteria, quality methods and the quality responsibilities of those involved.

When quality planning is neglected, the people involved in the project may have conflicting views on the scope of the solution, what constitutes a successful result, the approach to be adopted, the extent of the work required, who should be involved, and what the roles are.

● Quality control focuses on the operational techniques and activities used by those involved in the project to check that the products meet their quality criteria and to identify ways of eliminating causes of unsatisfactory performance.

Capturing and acting on lessons contributes to the PRINCE2 quality approach, as it is a means of achieving continual improvement.

To be following PRINCE2, a project must, as a minimum:

● define its quality management approach. This approach must minimally cover:

   ● the project's approach to quality control

   ● the project's approach to project assurance

   ● how the management of quality is communicated throughout the project lifecycle

   ● the roles and responsibilities for quality management (PRINCE2's defined roles and responsibilities principle)

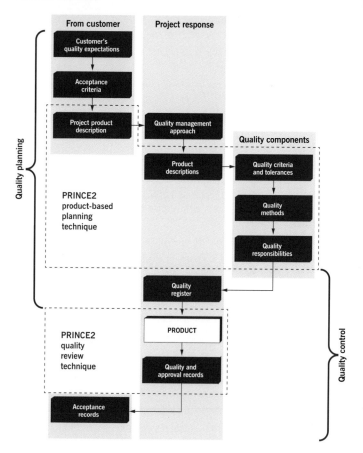

Figure 4.3 The quality audit trail

- specify explicit quality criteria for products in their product descriptions (PRINCE2's focus on products principle)
- maintain records to provide evidence that the planned quality activities have been carried out, and summarize those activities that are planned or have taken place in some form of quality register
- specify the customer's quality expectations and prioritized acceptance criteria for the project in the project product description (see section A.21)
- use lessons to inform quality planning, the definition of quality expectations and quality criteria (PRINCE2's learn from experience principle)
- produce and maintain two products:
  - quality management approach (see section A.22)
  - quality register (see section A.23).

4.4 The plans theme

Key message

The purpose of the plans theme is to facilitate communication and control by defining the means of delivering the products.

A plan enables the project team to understand:

- what products need to be delivered
- the risks (both opportunities and threats)
- any issues with the definition of scope

- which people, specialist equipment and resources are needed
- when activities and events should happen
- whether targets (for time, cost, quality, scope, risk and benefits) are achievable.

A plan provides a baseline against which progress can be measured and is the basis for securing support for the project, agreeing the scope and gaining commitment to provide the required resources.

PRINCE2's principle of manage by stages reflects that it is usually not possible to plan the whole project from the outset. Planning becomes more difficult and uncertain the further into the future it extends. There will be a time period over which it is possible to plan with reasonable accuracy; this is called the 'planning horizon'. It is seldom possible to plan with any degree of accuracy beyond the planning horizon.

PRINCE2 addresses the planning horizon issue by having both high-level and detailed plans. These are:

- a high-level project plan for the project as a whole. This will provide indicative timescales, milestones, cost and resource requirements based on estimates
- a detailed stage plan for each management stage, aligned with the overall project plan timescales. This plan must not extend beyond the planning horizon.

The very act of planning helps the project management team to think ahead to 'mentally rehearse the project'. It is such rehearsal that enables omissions, duplications, threats and opportunities to be identified and managed.

The plans need to be produced at different levels of scope and detail. PRINCE2 recommends three levels of plan (project, stage and team) to reflect the needs of the different levels of management involved in the project (see Figure 4.4).

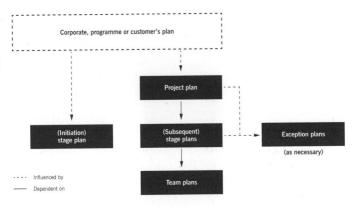

Figure 4.4 PRINCE2's planning levels

Should an exception occur, the affected plan is replaced by an exception plan.

To be following PRINCE2, a project must, as a minimum:

- ensure that plans enable the business case to be realized (PRINCE2's continued business justification principle)

- have at least two management stages: an initiation stage and at least one further management stage. The more complex and risky a project, the more management stages that will be required (PRINCE2's manage by stages principle)

- produce a project plan for the project as a whole and a stage plan for each management stage (PRINCE2's manage by stages principle)

- use product-based planning for the project plan, stage plans and exception plans. It may be optionally used for team plans

- produce specific plans for managing exceptions (PRINCE2's manage by exception principle)

- define the roles and responsibilities for planning (PRINCE2's defined roles and responsibilities principle)

- use lessons to inform planning (PRINCE2's learn from experience principle)

- produce and maintain the following products:

  - project product description (see section A.21)

  - product breakdown structure for each level of plan, with product descriptions (see section A.17)

  - plans at project, stage and team levels, and exception plans as required (see section A.16).

4.5 The risk theme

Key message

The purpose of the risk theme is to identify, assess and control uncertainty and, as a result, improve the ability of the project to succeed.

All projects encounter uncertainty when trying to achieve their objectives. This uncertainty may arise from events inside or outside the organization. For example, there may be uncertainty about the ability of the organization to agree the scope of the project within certain timescales or the availability of critical resources. There might also be uncertainty about the final scope and shape of legislation with which a project is required to ensure compliance.

Definition: Risk

A risk is an uncertain event or set of events that, should it occur, will have an effect on the achievement of objectives. A risk is measured by a combination of the probability of a perceived threat or opportunity occurring, and the magnitude of its impact on objectives.

Risks can have either a negative or positive impact on objectives if they occur. PRINCE2 uses the terms:

● **Threat** For uncertain events that would have a negative impact on objectives.

● **Opportunity** For uncertain events that would have a positive impact on objectives.

These can impact the project's objectives of delivering an agreed scope and benefits to an agreed time, cost and quality.

For risk management to be effective:

● risks that might affect the project achieving its objectives need to be identified, captured and described

● each risk needs to be assessed to understand its probability, impact and timing (proximity) so that it can be prioritized. The overall risk exposure needs to be kept under review, together with the impact of risk on the overall business justification for the project

- responses to each risk need to be planned, assigned to people to action and to own
- risk responses need to be implemented, monitored and controlled.

Information about risks must be communicated within the project and to stakeholders as a continual activity. Different organizations will have their own views on risk-taking that in turn dictate the overall amount of risk that they consider to be acceptable. This may be referred to as risk appetite.

PRINCE2 defines a number of different risk responses to opportunities and threats. These are as follows:

- **Threats** Avoid, reduce, transfer, share, accept or prepare contingent plans
- **Opportunities** Exploit, enhance, transfer (not often used), share, accept or prepare contingent plans

Definitions for each of these responses can be found in the glossary.

Not all opportunities may be taken up as there could be circumstances such as timing or cost which would have a negative impact on the project goals.

To be following PRINCE2, a project must, as a minimum:

- define its risk management approach, which must minimally cover:
  - how risks are identified and assessed, how risk management responses are planned and implemented, and how the management of risk is communicated throughout the project lifecycle
  - assessing whether identified risks might have a material impact on the business case (PRINCE2's continued business justification principle)

- the roles and responsibilities for risk management (PRINCE2's defined roles and responsibilities principle)
- maintain some form of risk register to record identified risks and decisions relating to their analysis, management and review
- ensure that project risks are identified, assessed, managed and reviewed throughout the project lifecycle
- use lessons to inform risk identification and management (PRINCE2's learn from experience principle)
- produce and maintain two products:
  - risk management approach (see section A.24)
  - risk register (see section A.25).

4.6 The change theme

Key message

The purpose of the change theme is to identify, assess and control any potential and approved changes to the project baselines.

Projects take place in their organizational environment and wider context, both of which change over time. It is rare that a project closes having delivered exactly what was envisaged when the project was initiated. It is often said that change is inevitable and this is certainly the case for long and more complex projects.

This means that projects need a systemic approach to the identification, assessment and control of issues that may result in change. Issue and change control is a continual activity, performed throughout the life of the project. Without an ongoing and effective issue and change control procedure, a project will either become unresponsive to its stakeholders or drift out of control.

In PRINCE2, changes are identified as 'issues'. PRINCE2 uses the term 'issue' to cover any relevant event that has happened, was not planned and requires management action. Issues may be raised at any time during the project by anyone with an interest in the project or its outcome.

The different types of issue that need to be dealt with during a project are:

- request for change
- off-specification
- problem/concern.

These terms are defined in the glossary.

To be following PRINCE2, a project must, as a minimum:

- define its change control approach. This approach must minimally cover:
  - how issues are identified and managed
  - assessing whether identified issues might have a material impact on the business case (PRINCE2's continued business justification principle)
  - the roles and responsibilities for change control (PRINCE2's defined roles and responsibilities principle), including a defined change authority
- define how product baselines are created, maintained and controlled
- maintain some form of issue register to record identified issues and decisions relating to their analysis, management and review

- ensure that project issues are captured, examined, managed and reviewed throughout the project lifecycle
- use lessons to inform issue identification and management (PRINCE2's learn from experience principle)
- produce and maintain two products:
  - issue register (see section A.12)
  - change control approach (see section A.3).

4.7 The progress theme

Key message

The purpose of the progress theme is to establish mechanisms to monitor and compare actual achievements against those planned; provide a forecast for the project objectives and the project's continued viability; and control any unacceptable deviations.

Progress is the measure of the achievement of the objectives of a plan. Controlling progress is central to project management, ensuring that the project remains viable against its approved business case. Progress control involves measuring actual progress against the performance targets of time, cost, quality, scope, benefits and risk. This information is used to make decisions such as whether to approve a management stage or work package, whether to escalate deviations, and whether to prematurely close the project and take actions as required. Progress can be monitored at work package, management stage and project levels.

Of PRINCE2's seven principles, the principle of manage by exception is particularly important to the progress theme. An exception is a situation where it can be forecast that there will be a deviation beyond agreed tolerance levels.

Tolerances are the permissible deviations above and below a plan's target for cost and time without escalating the deviation to the next level of management. There may also be tolerance levels for quality, scope, benefits and risk.

To be following PRINCE2, a project must, as a minimum:

● define its approach to controlling progress in the PID

● be managed by stages (PRINCE2's manage by stages principle)

● set tolerances and be managed by exception against these tolerances (PRINCE2's manage by exception principle)

● review the business justification when exceptions are raised (PRINCE2's continued business justification principle)

● learn lessons (PRINCE2's learn from experience principle).

● produce and maintain these products:

  ● issue register (see section A.12)

  ● product status account (if used) (see section A.18)

  ● quality register (see section A.23)

  ● risk register (see section A.25).

PRINCE2 provides progress control through:

● delegating authority from one level of management to the level below it

● dividing the project into management stages and authorizing the project one management stage at a time (PRINCE2's manage by stages principle)

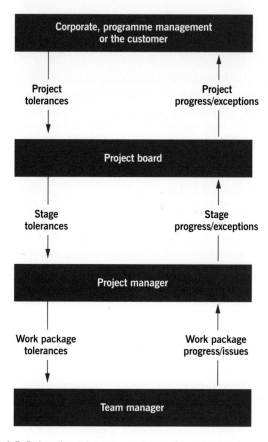

Figure 4.5 Delegating tolerances and reporting actual and forecast progress

- time-driven and event-driven progress reporting and reviews
- raising exceptions (PRINCE2's manage by exception principle).

The project's controls should be documented in the PID.

The allocation of tolerances is outlined in Figure 4.5. Tolerances are either set by or delegated to the following management levels:

- Corporate, programme management or the customer sits outside the project but sets the overall requirements and tolerance levels for the project.

- The project board has overall control at a project level, as long as forecasts remain within project tolerance, and will allocate tolerances for each management stage to the project manager.

- The project manager has day-to-day control for a management stage within the tolerance limits laid down by the project board.

- The team manager has control over a work package, but only within the work package tolerances agreed with the project manager.

5 Processes

PRINCE2 is a process-based approach for project management. A process is a structured set of activities designed to accomplish a specific objective. It takes one or more defined inputs and turns them into defined outputs.

There are seven processes in PRINCE2, which provide the set of activities required to direct, manage and deliver a project successfully. The processes address the flow of the project, with recommended actions relating to the different themes linked together.

Figure 5.1 shows how each process is used throughout a project's lifecycle. The lifecycle has three management stages: an initiation stage, subsequent stage(s), and the final stage. Note that on a simple project, there may only be two stages: an initiation stage and one delivery stage (the final stage).

As shown in Figure 1.1, PRINCE2 recognizes four levels of management:

- Corporate, programme management or the customer
- The project board
- The project manager
- The team manager.

PRINCE2 requires that project management processes are as simple as possible and that they reflect the needs of the project. There may be some activities, however, especially relating to governance, which need to be prescriptive. This can happen where they interface with higher-level processes within the organization, such as those for procurement or finance (when allocating funds at the start of a new stage, for example).

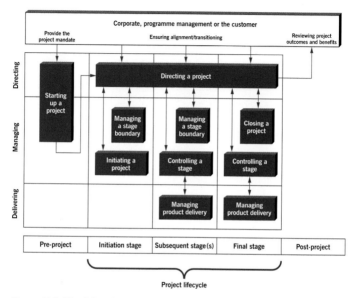

Figure 5.1 The PRINCE2 processes

For most projects, all processes remain relevant even for simple projects; what changes is the way in which they are undertaken, the activities and the degree of formality. Informality, with the right mindset, does not necessarily mean less rigour.

Processes can be tailored 'up' or 'down' (i.e. additional detailed documentation and discipline can be introduced for high-risk projects, whereas concise bullet-point presentations and more informal processes may be adequate for low-risk projects).

Key message

Tailoring allows the PRINCE2 process model to be adapted, revising the processes, activities, their sequencing and how the role responsibilities are allocated, provided that:

● the PRINCE2 principles are upheld

● the purpose and objectives of the process are not compromised.

5.1 Starting up a project

The purpose of the starting up a project process is to ensure that the prerequisites for initiating a project are in place by answering the question: Do we have a viable and worthwhile project? The decision to start the project must be explicit; the activities from starting up a project happen before this decision.

The objective of the process is to ensure that:

● there is a business justification and all necessary authorities exist for initiating the project

● sufficient information is available to define and confirm the scope of the project, the various ways the project can be delivered are evaluated, and a project approach is selected

● individuals are appointed who will undertake the work required in project initiation and/or will take significant project management roles in the project

● the work required for project initiation is planned

● time is not wasted because of unsound assumptions regarding the project's scope, timescales, acceptance criteria and constraints.

The activities in the process are to:

● appoint the executive and the project manager
● capture previous lessons
● design and appoint the project management team
● prepare the outline business case
● select the project approach and assemble the project brief
● plan the initiation stage.

5.2 Directing a project

The purpose of the directing a project process is to enable the project board to be accountable for the project's success by making key decisions and exercising overall control while delegating day-to-day management of the project to the project manager.

The objective of the process is to ensure that:

● there is authority to initiate the project, deliver the project's products and close the project
● management direction and control are provided throughout the project's lifecycle
● the project remains viable
● corporate, programme management or the customer has an interface to the project
● plans for realizing the post-project benefits are managed and reviewed.

The activities in the process are project board oriented and are to:

- authorize initiation
- authorize the project
- authorize a stage or exception plan
- give ad hoc direction
- authorize project closure.

5.3 Initiating a project

The purpose of the initiating a project process is to establish solid foundations for the project, enabling the organization to understand the work that needs to be done to deliver the project's products before committing to a significant spend.

Every PRINCE2 project has an initiation stage. The key deliverable from this stage is the PID, which includes an overall project plan and defines baselines for the six performance targets of time, cost, quality, scope, risk and benefits. The PID represents an authoritative statement of what the project will deliver, how this will be achieved, and by whom.

By the end of the process, there should be a common understanding of:

- the reasons for doing the project, the benefits expected and the associated risks
- the scope of what is to be done, how and when the products will be delivered, and at what cost
- who is to be involved in the decision-making, the information they need, and in what format and time
- how the quality required will be achieved
- how baselines will be established, and progress monitored and controlled

- how risks, issues and changes will be identified, assessed and controlled

- how the corporate, programme management or customer method will be tailored to suit the project.

The activities in the process are project manager oriented and are to:

- agree the tailoring requirements
- prepare the risk management approach
- prepare the change control approach
- prepare the quality management approach
- prepare the communication management approach
- set up the project controls
- create the project plan
- refine the business case
- assemble the project initiation documentation (PID).

5.4 Controlling a stage

The purpose of the controlling a stage process is to assign work to be done, monitor such work, deal with issues, report progress to the project board, and take corrective actions to ensure that the management stage remains within tolerance.

The objective of the process is to ensure that:

- attention is focused on delivery of the management stage's products. Any movement away from the direction and products agreed at the start of the management stage is monitored to avoid uncontrolled change and loss of focus

- risks and issues are kept under control

- the business case is kept under review
- the agreed products for the management stage are delivered to stated quality standards, within cost, effort and time agreed, and ultimately in support of the achievement of the defined benefits
- the project management team is focused on delivery within the tolerances laid down.

The activities in the process are project manager oriented and comprise:

- Work packages:
  - authorize a work package
  - review work package status
  - receive completed work packages
- Monitoring and reporting:
  - review the management stage status
  - report highlights
- Issues and risks:
  - capture and examine issues and risks
  - escalate issues and risks
  - take corrective action.

5.5 Managing product delivery

The purpose of the managing product delivery process is to control the link between the project manager and the team manager(s), by agreeing the requirements for acceptance, execution and delivery.

The role of the team manager(s) is to coordinate an area of work that will deliver one or more of the project's products. They can be internal or external to the customer's organization.

The objective of the process is to ensure that:

● work on products allocated to the team is authorized and agreed, and the planned products are delivered to expectations and within tolerance

● team managers, team members and suppliers are clear as to what is to be produced and what is the expected effort, cost or timescale

● accurate progress information is provided to the project manager at an agreed frequency to ensure that expectations are managed.

The activities in the process are team manager oriented and are to:

● accept a work package

● execute a work package

● deliver a work package.

5.6 Managing a stage boundary

The purpose of the managing a stage boundary process is to enable the project manager to provide the project board with sufficient information to be able to:

● review the success of the current management stage

● approve the next stage plan

● review the updated project plan

● confirm continued business justification and acceptability of the risks.

Therefore, the process should be executed at, or close to, the end of each management stage.

The objective of the process is to:

● assure the project board that all products in the stage plan for the current management stage have been completed and approved

- prepare the stage plan for the next management stage
- review and, if necessary, update the PID; in particular the business case, project plan, project approaches, project management team structure and role descriptions
- provide the information needed for the project board to assess the continuing viability of the project
- record any information that can help later management stages of this project and/or other projects
- request authorization to start the next management stage.

For a project in exception (when tolerances are forecast to be exceeded), the objectives of the process are to:

- review and, if necessary, update the PID; in particular the customer's quality expectations, project approaches and controls, and role descriptions
- provide the information needed for the project board to assess the continuing viability of the project
- prepare an exception plan as directed by the project board
- seek approval to replace the project plan or stage plan with the exception plan.

The activities in the process are project manager oriented and are to:

- plan the next management stage
- update the project plan
- update the business case
- report management stage end
- produce an exception plan.

5.7 Closing a project

The purpose of the closing a project process is to provide a fixed point at which acceptance of the project's product is confirmed, and to recognize that objectives set out in the original PID have been achieved (or approved changes to the objectives have been achieved), or that the project has nothing more to contribute.

The objective of the process is to:

- verify user acceptance of the project's products
- ensure that the host site is able to support the products when the project is disbanded
- review the performance of the project against its baselines
- assess any benefits that have already been realized and update the benefits management approach to include any post-project benefit reviews
- ensure that provision has been made to address all open issues and risks, with follow-on action recommendations.

The activities in the process are project manager oriented and are to:

- prepare planned closure
- prepare premature closure
- hand over products
- evaluate the project
- recommend project closure.

6 Considerations for organizational adoption

For those organizations adopting PRINCE2, the considerations are:

- tailoring PRINCE2 to create an organization's method
- embedding the tailored method within the organization.

6.1 Tailoring PRINCE2 to create an organization's method

Apart from the PRINCE2 principles, all other elements of PRINCE2 can be tailored to fit with the organization's existing governance arrangements. Before creating a project management method, it is important to understand why the organization wants to do this. By understanding the drivers and objectives, it is more likely that the method created will meet the needs of the organization.

The extent to which an organization can tailor its project management method will be influenced by:

- the rules or guidelines that are applicable to the organization
- the degrees of freedom that each role holder is allowed
- who 'approves' the tailoring
- who can advise people on tailoring.

6.2 Embedding the tailored method within the organization

Embedding the tailored method within the organization's working practices and ensuring its widespread use involves changing the way that people work, so that the outcome (widespread use) can be realized, leading to a higher project success rate and enhanced business performance.

Current approaches to change management combine the psychological and engineering views of the world to create repeatable change methods, drawing on a wide range of tools and techniques. The application of different change methods has implications for the way organizations and their leaders regard change, the way they manage change and even the effectiveness of any change initiatives. At the heart of most change models is gaining the support of those who are required to change their ways of working.

To gain stakeholder support, change management approaches should not just involve training, but may also include coaching, mentoring, stakeholder engagement, marketing and communications activities to embed a real understanding of the need for the change and the resulting benefits. Change is as much about managing people's expectations and perceptions as managing facts.

Appendix A: PRINCE2's management products

PRINCE2 defines a set of management products that will be required as part of managing the project and establishing and maintaining quality. These management products are not necessarily text documents; rather, they are information sets that are used by the PRINCE2 processes and which can be tailored to the requirements and environment of each project. This tailoring may include their composition, format, quality criteria and naming.

Management products can be documents, slides, spreadsheets or data in information systems which are brought together, either on screen or as outputs, to form reports.

Some management products may not be used unless there is a specific requirement for the additional information they provide. These are:

- configuration item record
- lessons report
- product status account.

Types of management product

There are three types of management product: baselines, records and reports.

Baseline management products are those that define aspects of the project and, when approved, are subject to change control. These are:

- A.1 Benefits management approach
- A.2 Business case
- A.3 Change control approach
- A.5 Communication management approach

- A.16 Plan (covers project plans, stage plans, exception plans and, optionally, team plans)
- A.17 Product description
- A.19 Project brief
- A.20 Project initiation documentation (PID)
- A.21 Project product description
- A.22 Quality management approach
- A.24 Risk management approach
- A.26 Work package.

Records are dynamic management products that maintain information regarding project progress. These are:

- A.6 Configuration item record
- A.7 Daily log
- A.12 Issue register
- A.14 Lessons log
- A.23 Quality register
- A.25 Risk register.

Reports are management products providing a snapshot of the status of certain aspects of the project. They do not need to be documents. They could be emails, notes of meetings, wall charts or entries in a daily log. Where verbal reports are used, the information could be incorporated in other reports. PRINCE2 reports are:

- A.4 Checkpoint report
- A.8 End project report
- A.9 End stage report
- A.10 Exception report

- A.11 Highlight report
- A.13 Issue report
- A.15 Lessons report
- A.18 Product status account.

Although records and reports are not subject to change control, they are still subject to other aspects of configuration management, such as version control, safe storage, access rights, etc.

A.1 Benefits management approach

A benefits management approach defines the benefits management actions and benefits reviews that will be put in place to ensure that the project's outcomes are achieved and confirm that project's benefits are realized. If the project is part of a programme, the benefits management approach may be contained within the programme's benefits realization plan and executed at the programme level. Post-project, the benefits management approach is maintained and executed by corporate, programme management or the customer.

A.2 Business case

A business case is used to document the business justification for undertaking a project, based on the estimated costs (of development, implementation and incremental ongoing operations and maintenance costs) against the anticipated benefits to be gained and offset by any associated risks. It should outline how and when the anticipated benefits can be measured.

The outline business case is developed in the starting up a project process and refined by the initiating a project process. The directing a project process covers the approval and re-affirmation of the business case. The business case is used by the controlling a stage process when assessing impacts of issues and risks. It is reviewed and updated at the end of each management stage by the managing a stage boundary process, and at the end of the project by the closing a project process.

A.3 Change control approach

A change control approach is used to identify, assess and control any potential and approved changes to the project baselines. It describes the procedures, techniques and standards to be applied and the responsibilities for achieving an effective issue management and change control procedure.

A.4 Checkpoint report

A checkpoint report is used to report, at a frequency defined in the work package, the status of the work package.

A.5 Communication management approach

A communication management approach contains a description of the means and frequency of communication with parties both internal and external to the project. It facilitates engagement with stakeholders through the establishment of a controlled and bidirectional flow of information.

A.6 Configuration item record

Configuration item records are only created if required by the project's change control approach. Their purpose is to provide a record of such information as the history, status, version and variant of each configuration item, and any details of important relationships between them. The set of configuration item records for a project is often referred to as a configuration library.

A.7 Daily log

A daily log may be used to record informal issues, required actions or significant events not captured by other PRINCE2 registers or logs. It can act as the project diary for the project manager. It can also be used as a repository for issues and risks during the starting up a project process if the other registers have not been set up.

A.8 End project report

An end project report is used during project closure to review how the project performed against the version of the PID used to authorize it.

A.9 End stage report

An end stage report is used to give a summary of progress to date, the overall project situation, and sufficient information to ask for a project board decision on what to do next with the project. The project board uses the information in the end stage report in tandem with the next stage plan to decide what action to take with the project: for example, authorize the next stage, amend the project scope or stop the project.

A.10 Exception report

An exception report is produced when a stage plan or project plan is forecast to exceed tolerance levels set. It is prepared by the project manager in order to inform the project board of the situation, and to offer options and recommendations for the way to proceed.

A.11 Highlight report

A highlight report is used to provide the project board (and possibly other stakeholders) with a summary of the management stage status at intervals defined by them. The project board uses the report to monitor management stage and project progress. The project manager also uses it to advise the project board of any potential problems or areas where the project board could help.

A.12 Issue register

The purpose of the issue register is to capture and maintain information on all the issues that are being formally managed. The issue register should be monitored by the project manager on a regular basis.

A.13 Issue report

An issue report is a report containing the description, impact assessment and recommendations for a request for change, off-specification or a problem/concern. It is created only for those issues that need to be handled formally.

A.14 Lessons log

The lessons log is a project repository for lessons that apply to this project or future projects. Some lessons may originate from other projects and should be captured on the lessons log for input to the project's approaches and plans. Some lessons may originate from within the project, where new experience (both good and bad) can be passed on to others.

A.15 Lessons report

A lessons report may be produced to support the lessons log if more information is required. It can be used to pass on any lessons that can be usefully applied to other projects. The purpose of the report is to provoke action so that the positive lessons become embedded in the organization's way of working, and the organization is able to avoid any negative lessons on future projects.

A.16 Plan

A plan provides a statement of how and when objectives are to be achieved, by showing the major products, activities and resources required for the scope of the plan. In PRINCE2, there are three levels of plan: project, stage and team. Team plans are optional and may not need to follow the same composition as a project plan or stage plan. An exception plan is created at the same level as the plan that it is replacing.

A plan should cover not just the activities to create products but also the activities to manage product creation, including activities for assurance, quality management, risk management, change control, communication and any other project controls required.

A.17 Product description

A product description is used to:

- understand the detailed nature, purpose, function and appearance of the product
- define who will use the product
- identify the sources of information or supply for the product
- identify the level of quality required of the product
- enable identification of activities to produce, review and approve the product
- define the people or skills required to produce, review and approve the product.

A.18 Product status account

If required by the project's change control approach, a product status account is used to provide information about the state of products within defined limits. The limits can vary. For example, the report could cover the entire project, a particular management stage, a particular area of the project or the history of a specific product. It is particularly useful if the project manager wishes to confirm the version number of products.

A.19 Project brief

A project brief is used to provide a full and firm foundation for the initiation of the project and is created in the starting up a project process. In the initiating a project process, the contents of the project brief are extended and refined in the PID, after which the project brief is no longer maintained.

A.20 Project initiation documentation (PID)

The purpose of the PID is to define the project, in order to form the basis for its management and an assessment of its overall success. The PID gives the direction and scope of the project and (along with the stage plan) forms the 'contract' between the project manager and the project board.

The three primary uses of the PID are to:

- ensure that the project has a sound basis before asking the project board to make any major commitment to the project
- act as a base document against which the project board and project manager can assess progress, issues and ongoing viability questions
- provide a single source of reference about the project so that people joining the 'temporary organization' can quickly and easily find out what the project is about, and how it is being managed.

The PID is a living product in that it should always reflect the current status, plans and controls of the project. Its component products will need to be updated and re-baselined, as necessary, at the end of each management stage, to reflect the current status of its constituent parts.

A.21 Project product description

The project product description is a special form of product description that defines what the project must deliver in order to gain acceptance. It is used to:

- gain agreement from the user on the project's scope and requirements
- define the customer's quality expectations
- define the acceptance criteria, method and responsibilities for the project.

The product description for the project product is created in the starting up a project process as part of the initial scoping activity, and is refined during the initiating a project process when creating the project plan. It is subject to formal change control and should be checked at management stage boundaries (during managing a stage boundary) to see if any changes are required. It is used by the closing a project process as part of the verification that the project has delivered what was expected of it, and that the acceptance criteria have been met.

A.22 Quality management approach

A quality management approach describes how quality will be managed on the project. This includes the specific processes, procedures, techniques, standards and responsibilities to be applied.

A.23 Quality register

A quality register is used to summarize all the quality management activities that are planned or have taken place, and provides information for the end stage reports and end project report. Its purpose is to:

- issue a unique reference for each quality activity
- act as a pointer to the quality records for a product

- act as a summary of the number and type of quality activities undertaken.

A.24 Risk management approach

A risk management approach describes how risk will be managed on the project. This includes the specific processes, procedures, techniques, standards and responsibilities to be applied.

A.25 Risk register

A risk register provides a record of identified risks relating to the project, including their status and history. It is used to capture and maintain information on all the identified threats and opportunities relating to the project.

A.26 Work package

A work package is a set of information about one or more required products collated by the project manager to pass responsibility for work or delivery formally to a team manager or team member.

Appendix C: Roles and responsibilities

Note: there is no Appendix B. This appendix has been numbered to reflect the system used in the main volume, *Managing Successful Projects with PRINCE2* (2017 edition).

These roles may be tailored to meet the needs of the project and some roles can be shared or combined as long as the minimum requirements for the organization theme are met.

C.1 Project board

The project board is accountable to corporate, programme management or the customer for the success of the project, and has the authority to direct the project within the remit set by corporate, programme management or the customer as documented in the project mandate.

The project board is also responsible for the communications between the project management team and stakeholders external to that team (e.g. corporate, programme management or the customer).

According to the scale, complexity, importance and risk of the project, project board members may delegate some project assurance tasks to separate individuals. The project board may also delegate decisions regarding changes to a change authority.

C.2 Executive

The executive is ultimately accountable for the project, supported by the senior user and senior supplier. The executive's role is to ensure that the project is focused throughout its life on achieving its objectives and delivering a product that will achieve the forecast benefits. The executive has to ensure that the project gives value for money, ensuring a cost-conscious approach to the project, balancing the demands of the business, user and supplier.

Throughout the project, the executive is responsible for the business case.

The project board is not a democracy controlled by votes. The executive is the ultimate decision maker and is supported in the decision-making by the senior user and senior supplier.

C.3 Senior user

The senior user is responsible for specifying the needs of those who will use the project's products, for user liaison with the project management team, and for monitoring that the solution will meet those needs within the constraints of the business case in terms of quality, functionality and ease of use.

The role represents the interests of all those who will use the project's products (including operations and maintenance), those for whom the products will achieve an objective or those who will use the products to deliver benefits. The senior user role commits user resources and monitors products against requirements. This role may require more than one person to cover all the user interests. For the sake of effectiveness, the role should not be split between too many people.

The senior user specifies the benefits and is held to account by demonstrating to corporate, programme management or the customer that the forecast benefits which were the basis of project approval have in fact been realized. This is likely to involve a commitment beyond the end of the life of the project.

C.4 Senior supplier

The senior supplier represents the interests of those designing, developing, facilitating, procuring and implementing the project's products. This role is accountable for the quality of products delivered by the supplier(s) and is responsible for the technical integrity of the project. If necessary, more than one person may represent the suppliers.

Depending on the particular customer/supplier environment, the customer may also wish to appoint an independent person or group to carry out assurance on the supplier's products (e.g. if the relationship between the customer and supplier is a commercial one).

C.5 Project manager

The project manager is accountable to the project board, and ultimately the executive, and has the authority to run the project on a day-to-day basis, within the constraints laid down by them.

The project manager's prime responsibility is to ensure that the project produces the required products within the specified tolerances of time, cost, quality, scope, benefits and risk. The project manager is also responsible for the project producing a result capable of achieving the benefits defined in the business case.

C.6 Team manager

The team manager's prime responsibility is to ensure production of those products defined by the project manager to an appropriate quality, in a set timescale and at a cost acceptable to the project board. The team manager is accountable to, and takes direction from, the project manager.

C.7 Project assurance

Project assurance covers the primary stakeholder interests (business, user and supplier). The role has to be independent of the project manager; therefore the project board cannot delegate any of its assurance activities to the project manager.

C.8 Change authority

The project board may delegate authority for approving responses to requests for change or off-specifications to a separate individual or group, called a change authority. The project manager could be assigned as the change authority for some aspects of the project (e.g. changing baselined work packages if it does not affect management stage tolerances).

C.9 Project support

The provision of any project support on a formal basis is optional. If it is not delegated to a separate person or function, it will need to be undertaken by the project manager.

One support function that must be considered is that of change control. Depending on the project size and environment, there may be a need to formalize this and it may become a task with which the project manager cannot cope without support.

Project support functions may be provided by a project office or by specific resources for the project. For further information on the use of a project office, see the AXELOS publication, *Portfolio, Programme and Project Offices*.

Glossary

This glossary only includes terms mentioned in the handbook. Management products and roles are described in Appendices A and C and their definitions are not included here. For the full set of PRINCE2 glossary definitions, see *Managing Successful Projects with PRINCE2*.

accept (risk response)

A risk response that means that the organization takes the chance that the risk will occur, with full impact on objectives if it does.

acceptance

The formal act of acknowledging that the project has met agreed acceptance criteria and thereby met the requirements of its stakeholders.

acceptance criteria

A prioritized list of criteria that the project product must meet before the customer will accept it (i.e. measurable definitions of the attributes required for the set of products to be acceptable to key stakeholders).

activity

A process, function or task that occurs over time, has recognizable results and is managed. It is usually defined as part of a process or plan.

agile and agile methods

A broad term for a collection of behaviours, frameworks, concepts and techniques that go together to enable teams and individuals to work in an agile way that is typified by collaboration, prioritization, iterative and incremental delivery, and timeboxing. There are several specific methods (or frameworks) that are classed as agile, such as Scrum and Kanban. PRINCE2 is completely compatible with working in an agile way.

approval

The formal confirmation that a product is complete and meets its requirements (less any concessions) as defined by its product description.

assurance

All the systematic actions necessary to provide confidence that the target (e.g. system, process, organization, programme, project, outcome, benefit, capability, product output or deliverable) is appropriate. Appropriateness might be defined subjectively or objectively in different circumstances. The implication is that assurance will have a level of independence from that which is being assured.

authority

The right to allocate resources and make decisions (applies to project, management stage and team levels).

avoid (risk response)

A risk response to a threat where the threat either can no longer have an impact or can no longer happen.

baseline

Reference levels against which an entity is monitored and controlled.

baseline management product

A type of management product that defines aspects of the project and, when approved, is subject to change control.

benefit

The measurable improvement resulting from an outcome perceived as an advantage by one or more stakeholders.

change control

The procedure that ensures that all changes that may affect the project's agreed objectives are identified, assessed and then approved, rejected or deferred.

checkpoint

A team-level, time-driven review of progress.

configuration item

An entity that is subject to change control. The entity may be a component of a product, a product or a set of products in a release.

configuration management

Technical and administrative activities concerned with the controlled change of a product.

constraints

The restrictions or limitations by which the project is bound.

contingent plan

A plan intended for use only if required (e.g. if a risk response is not successful). Often called a fallback plan.

corrective action

A set of actions to resolve a threat to a plan's tolerances or a defect in a product.

customer

The person or group who commissioned the work and will benefit from the end results.

customer's quality expectations

A statement about the quality expected from the project product, captured in the project product description.

deliverable

See output.

dis-benefit

A measurable decline resulting from an outcome perceived as negative by one or more stakeholders, which reduces one or more organizational objective(s).

embedding (PRINCE2)

The act of making something an integral part of a bigger whole.

Embedding is what an organization needs to do to adopt PRINCE2 as its corporate project management method and encourage its widespread use.

enhance (risk response)

A risk response to an opportunity where proactive actions are taken to enhance both the probability of the event occurring and the impact of the event should it occur.

event-driven control

A control that takes place when a specific event occurs. This could be, for example, the end of a management stage, the completion of the PID, or the creation of an exception report. It could also include organizational events that may affect the project, such as the end of the financial year.

exception

A situation where it can be forecast that there will be a deviation beyond the tolerance levels agreed between the project manager and the project board (or between the project board and corporate, programme management or the customer).

exception plan

A plan that often follows an exception report. For a stage plan exception, it covers the period from the present to the end of the current management stage. If the exception were at project level, the project plan would be replaced.

exploit (risk response)

A risk response to an opportunity. It means seizing the opportunity to ensure that it will happen and that the impact will be realized.

governance (corporate)

The ongoing activity of maintaining a sound system of internal control by which the directors and officers of an organization ensure that effective management systems, including financial monitoring and control systems, have been put in place to protect assets, earning capacity and the reputation of the organization.

governance (project)

Those areas of corporate governance that are specifically related to project activities. Effective governance of project management ensures that an organization's project portfolio is aligned with the organization's objectives, is delivered efficiently and is sustainable.

impact (of risk)

The result of a particular threat or opportunity actually occurring, or the anticipation of such a result.

initiation stage

The period from when the project board authorizes initiation to when it authorizes the project (or decides not to go ahead with it). The detailed planning and establishment of the project management infrastructure is covered by the initiating a project process.

issue

A relevant event that has happened, was not planned, and requires management action. It can be any concern, query, request for change, suggestion or off-specification raised during a project. Project issues can be about anything to do with the project.

log

An informal repository managed by the project manager that does not require any agreement by the project board on its format and composition. PRINCE2 has two logs: the daily log and the lessons log.

management product

A product that will be required as part of managing the project, and establishing and maintaining quality (e.g. highlight report, end stage report). The management products are constant, whatever the type of project, and can be used as described, or with any relevant modifications, for all projects. There are three types of management product: baselines, records and reports.

management stage

The section of a project that the project manager is managing on behalf of the project board at any one time, at the end of which the project board will wish to review progress to date, the state of the project plan, the business case and risks and the next stage plan, in order to decide whether to continue with the project.

maturity

A measure of the reliability, efficiency and effectiveness of a process, function, organization, etc. The most mature processes and functions are formally aligned with business objectives and strategy, and are supported by a framework for continual improvement.

maturity model

A method of assessing organizational capability in a given area of skill.

milestone

A significant event in a plan's schedule, such as completion of key work packages, a development step or a management stage.

off-specification

Something that should be provided by the project, but currently is not (or is forecast not to be). It might be a missing product or a product not meeting its specifications. It is one type of issue.

outcome

The result of change, normally affecting real-world behaviour and/or circumstances. Outcomes are desired when a change is conceived. They are achieved as a result of the activities undertaken to effect the change.

output

A specialist product that is handed over to a user (or users). Note that management products are not outputs but are created solely for the purpose of managing the project.

performance targets

A plan's goals for time, cost, quality, scope, benefits and risk.

planning horizon

The period of time for which it is possible to plan accurately.

portfolio

The totality of an organization's investment (or segment thereof) in the changes required to achieve its strategic objectives.

PRINCE2 principles

The guiding obligations for good project management practice that form the basis of a project being managed using PRINCE2.

PRINCE2 project

A project that applies the PRINCE2 principles.

probability

This is the evaluated likelihood of a particular threat or opportunity actually happening, including a consideration of the frequency with which this may arise.

problem

A type of issue (other than a request for change or off-specification) that the project manager needs to resolve or escalate. Also known as a concern.

procedure

A series of actions for a particular aspect of project management established specifically for the project (e.g. a risk management procedure).

process

A structured set of activities designed to accomplish a specific objective. A process takes one or more defined inputs and turns them into defined outputs.

product

An input or output, whether tangible or intangible, that can be described in advance, created and tested. PRINCE2 has two types of products: management products and specialist products.

product breakdown structure

A hierarchy of all the products to be produced during a plan.

programme

A temporary, flexible organization structure created to coordinate, direct and oversee the implementation of a set of related projects and activities in order to deliver outcomes and benefits related to the organization's strategic objectives. A programme is likely to have a life that spans several years.

project

A temporary organization that is created for the purpose of delivering one or more business products according to an agreed business case.

project lifecycle

The period from initiation of a project to the acceptance of the project product.

project management

The planning, delegating, monitoring and control of all aspects of the project, and the motivation of those involved, to achieve the project objectives within the expected performance targets for time, cost, quality, scope, benefits and risk.

project management team

The entire management structure of the project board, and the project manager, plus any team manager, project assurance and project support roles.

project management team structure

An organization chart showing the people assigned to the project management team roles to be used, and their delegation and reporting relationships.

project mandate

An external product generated by the authority commissioning the project that forms the trigger for starting up a project.

project office

A temporary office set up to support the delivery of a specific change initiative being delivered as a project. If used, the project office undertakes the responsibility of the project support role.

project plan

A high-level plan showing the major products of the project, when they will be delivered and at what cost. An initial project plan is presented as part of the PID. This is revised as information on actual progress appears. It is a major control document for the project board to measure actual progress against expectations.

project product

What the project must deliver in order to gain acceptance.

proximity (of risk)

The time factor of risk (i.e. when the risk may occur). The impact of a risk may vary in severity depending on when the risk occurs.

quality

The degree to which a set of inherent characteristics of a product, service, process, person, organization, system or resource fulfils requirements.

quality control

The process of monitoring specific project results to determine whether they comply with relevant standards and of identifying ways to eliminate causes of unsatisfactory performance.

quality criteria

A description of the quality specification that the product must meet, and the quality measurements that will be applied by those inspecting the finished product.

quality management

The coordinated activities to direct and control an organization with regard to quality.

quality records

Evidence kept to demonstrate that the required quality assurance and quality control activities have been carried out.

records

Dynamic management products that maintain information regarding project progress.

reduce (risk response)

A response to a risk where proactive actions are taken to reduce the probability of the event occurring by performing some form of control, and/or to reduce the impact of the event should it occur.

registers

Formal repositories managed by the project manager that require agreement by the project board on their format, composition and use. PRINCE2 has three registers: issue register, risk register and quality register.

reports

Management products providing a snapshot of the status of certain aspects of the project.

request for change

A proposal for a change to a baseline. It is a type of issue.

risk

An uncertain event or set of events that, should it occur, will have an effect on the achievement of objectives. A risk is measured by a combination of the probability of a perceived threat or opportunity occurring, and the magnitude of its impact on objectives.

risk appetite

An organization's unique attitude towards risk-taking that in turn dictates the amount of risk that it considers acceptable.

risk exposure

The extent of risk borne by the organization at the time.

risk management

The systematic application of principles, approaches and processes to the tasks of identifying and assessing risks, planning and implementing risk responses and communicating risk management activities with stakeholders.

risk response

Actions that may be taken to bring a situation to a level where exposure to risk is acceptable to the organization. These responses fall into a number of risk response categories.

risk tolerance

The threshold levels of risk exposure that, with appropriate approvals, can be exceeded, but which when exceeded will trigger some form of response (e.g. reporting the situation to senior management for action).

scope

For a plan, the sum total of its products and the extent of their requirements. It is described by the product breakdown structure for the plan and associated product descriptions.

share (risk response)

A risk response to either a threat or an opportunity through the application of a pain/gain formula: both parties share the gain (within pre-agreed limits) if the cost is less than the cost plan, and both share the pain (again within pre-agreed limits) if the cost plan is exceeded.

specialist product

A product whose development is the subject of the plan. The specialist products are specific to an individual project (e.g. an advertising campaign, a car park ticketing system, foundations for a building or a new business process). Also known as a deliverable. *See also* output.

sponsor

The main driving force behind a programme or project. PRINCE2 does not define a role for the sponsor, but the sponsor is most likely to be the executive on the project board, or the person who has appointed the executive.

stage

See management stage.

stage plan

A detailed plan used as the basis for project management control throughout a management stage.

stakeholder

Any individual, group or organization that can affect, be affected by or perceive itself to be affected by, an initiative (i.e. a programme, project, activity or risk).

supplier

The person, group or groups responsible for the supply of the project's specialist products.

tailoring

Adapting a method or process to suit the situation in which it will be used.

team plan

An optional level of plan used as the basis for team management control when executing work packages.

theme

An aspect of project management that needs to be continually addressed, and that requires specific treatment for the PRINCE2 processes to be effective.

threat

An uncertain event that could have a negative impact on objectives or benefits.

time-driven control

A management control that is periodic in nature, to enable the next higher authority to monitor progress (e.g. a control that takes place every 2 weeks). PRINCE2 offers two key time-driven progress reports: checkpoint report and highlight report.

tolerance

The permissible deviation above and below a plan's target for time and cost without escalating the deviation to the next level of management. There may also be tolerance levels for quality, scope, benefits and risk. Tolerance is applied at project, management stage and team levels.

transfer (risk response)

A response to a threat where a third party takes on responsibility for some of the financial impact of the threat (e.g. through insurance or by means of appropriate clauses in a contract).

user

The person or group who will use one or more of the project's products.

variant

A variation of a baselined product. For example, an operations manual may have English and Spanish variants.

version

A specific baseline of a product. Versions typically use naming conventions that enable the sequence or date of the baseline to be identified. For example, project plan version 2 is the baseline after project plan version 1.